# WORKBOOK

## FOR

# HOW TO MAKE
# MONEY IN STOCKS

A Winning System in Good Times and Bad
(Fourth Edition)

## Krystal Reads

# This workbook belong to

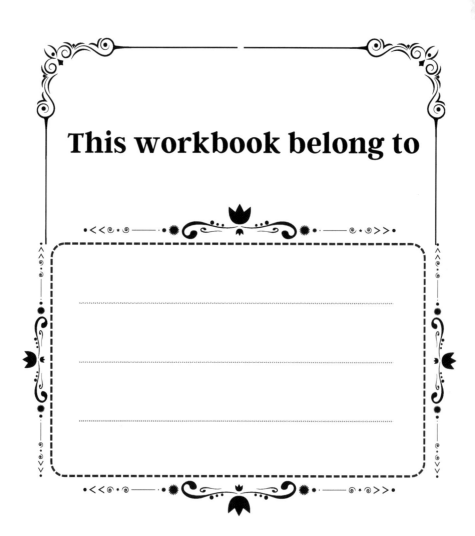

# Copyright © by Krystal Reads 2024

# How To Use This Workbook

Congrats for selecting this Workbook of "How to Make Money in Stocks: A Winning System in Good Times and Bad"! This manual is intended to improve your investing experience and turn abstract concepts into real-world financial gains. To get the most out of this worksheet, do the following:

1. ENGAGE IN ACTIVE READING: To start, read William O'Neil's "How to Make Money in Stocks" cover to cover in order to understand the fundamental ideas and techniques.

2. COMPREHENSIVE SYNOPSIS OF THE BOOK: This Workbook Summarizes the main book based on 7 key Ideas of the main book. With each key IDEA is represent a chapter. Get acquainted with the chapter summaries in this workbook before beginning the activities. Your recollection of the main ideas will be refreshed by this brief review.

3. ENGAGING IN EXERCISE: Take a close look at each chapter's specific activities. These exercises, which give real-world applications of the tactics discussed in the book, are taken straight from O'Neil's lectures.

4. A SPECIALIZED WRITING AREA: Make use of the large space given to write down your answers to each task. Make sure your ideas are well-captured while you're filling in tables, answering diary questions, or artistically expressing your observations.

5. REGULAR INTROSPECTION: Include this workbook in your everyday activities. Regularly review the exercises and evaluate how the techniques fit into your specific investing objectives.

6. ARTISTIC EXPRESSION: Go ahead and use your imagination! To improve your comprehension and make studying more fun, use workout forms such as coloring papers and drawn lines.

7. MONITOR DEVELOPMENT: Review your answers from time to time to monitor your development. Observe how your investing methods change over time and pinpoint areas that need work.

8. PRACTICAL TAKEAWAYS: Keep in mind that this workbook emphasizes action above just passive learning. Use the knowledge you get from each activity to inform your actual investing choices.

9. INTEGRATE WITH THE ORIGINAL BOOK: Use "How to Make Money in Stocks" in conjunction with this workbook for a whole educational experience. Compare your notes with the text to make sure you understand the important points.

10. YOUR INDIVIDUAL HANDBOOK: Use this workbook as a personal financial success guide. Your commitment to making frequent use of this resource will greatly improve your ability to make investments.

LAST THOUGHT

This workbook is meant to be a constant companion on your financial journey—it is not meant to be read once. Its effectiveness depends on your dedication to active participation. It is designed to assist you in internalizing the techniques. Make the most of every workout and see the development of your investing savvy as you follow the guidelines in "How to Make Money in Stocks.

# INTRODUCTION

## UNCOVER THE KEYS TO REALIZING SUBSTANTIAL PROFITS IN THE STOCK MARKET.

It might be intimidating for a lot of people to consider investing in stocks. Anxiety may be brought on by worries about future market downturns and the possibility of losing all of one's investment. Historical occurrences like the 1929 stock market collapse and the dotcom boom, which were both accompanied by widespread fear and hysteria, demonstrate how unpredictable the stock market can be.

There is a method for navigating this ambiguity, however. There are tried-and-true strategies to assist you in choosing excellent businesses, scheduling your investments wisely, and avoiding losses. Through historical stock market success and failure, you may create techniques that maximize your gains while minimizing prospective losses. You will examine some of these successful strategies in the sections that follow, which cover anything from finding important patterns in stock charts to figuring out which firms are the most likely to be profitable investments.

During this Investigation, you will learn about:

- The meaning of the phrase "cup with handle" in the stock market.
- similarities between businesses such as General Motors and Cisco Systems.
- How businesses that are genuinely inventive may outperform their rivals.

**Date:**

## Goals

# CHAPTER 1

## UNDERSTANDING ESSENTIAL CHART PATTERNS FOR SUCCESSFUL INVESTING

A secret to successful investment in the volatile realm of the stock market, where fortunes are made and lost, may be identified in historical trends. This gets us to our first important point: mastering the patterns seen in stock charts, with a focus on one particular pattern that has shown to be reliable over time.

A few things have been consistent throughout the stock market's history. Certain equities see dramatic price increases, others have sharp declines, and some just plod along unprofitably. The lesson here is that insightful information may be extracted and applied to current investing strategies by examining the performance of historical equities, from Apple in the 21st century to the Northern Pacific Railway in the early 20th century.

You have to become good at reading stock charts in order to do this. The core idea is rather evident: Become familiar with stock chart patterns, concentrating on just one kind of pattern.

Analyzing the state of affairs is essential for making wise judgments in many different domains. Physicians use diagnostic imaging methods such as MRIs and X-rays to identify diseases in their early stages, while geologists use seismic data to interpret earthquakes and find undiscovered oil sources.

Similar to this, knowing historical trends in the field of investment may help direct current decisions. Unless one is really lucky, failing to do so may result in financial losses.

What therefore ought investors search for on stock charts? Price patterns hold the key to the solution. The "Cup with Handle" is one of the most notable patterns. Typically, this pattern develops when a stock rises, falls, and then curves downward to create the base, or "cup." This base is important because it shows a strong group of investors that have faith in the company. If there is no support, the stock might crash. But with a strong foundation, the stock is well-positioned to gain should its circumstances shift. The next step makes the opposite side of the cup, with an ascent, and a dip creating the "handle." This is the exact moment when astute investors need to think about getting into the market. Stocks that follow this trend almost always see a later upswing in value.

Throughout the years, investors have profited handsomely from this dependable stock-market trend, whether they are studying the rise of Apple in the 2000s or Sea Containers in the 1970s. Investors may enhance their chances of success in their investment pursuits by strategically positioning themselves in the market by comprehending and implementing these ideas.

# Key Lessons

**Lesson 1 :** <u>**Opening Eternal Patterns to Make Well-Informed Decisions**</u>

To make well-informed decisions, identify the enduring trends in the history of the stock market.

**Lesson 2 :** <u>**Learning the Pattern of the "Cup with Handle":**</u>

Learn how to interpret stock charts, paying particular attention to the powerful "Cup with Handle" pattern.

**Lesson 3 :** <u>**Establishing a Robust Basis with Investors**</u>

Recognize the importance of a robust investor base as the cornerstone of a successful stock.

**Lesson 4 :** <u>**Strategic Alignment using Historical Perspectives:**</u>

Utilize past data to place yourself in the market strategically and increase the return on your investments.

### <u>Focus on Patterns</u>

Create a methodical framework for identifying and interpreting stock chart patterns.

<u>NOTE</u>

### <u>Creating a Sturdy Foundation</u>

Before making an investment, create a checklist to assess the strength of the investor base.

<u>NOTE</u>

### The Knowledge Journey

Create a plan for ongoing education regarding past stock market movements that includes a variety of educational tools.

<u>NOTE</u>

| Goals | Action Plan |
| --- | --- |
|  |  |
|  |  |
|  |  |
|  |  |
|  |  |
|  |  |
|  |  |
|  |  |
|  |  |

## Final Results

Have you looked into past stock
market trends to see what makes
some trends work and what
doesn't?

_____

_____

_____

_____

_____

_____

_____

Do you know what the "Cup with
Handle" pattern means while
investing in the stock market?

_____

_____

_____

_____

_____

_____

How often do you examine stock
charts before deciding which
investments to make?

_____

_____

_____

_____

_____

_____

Do you understand how crucial a robust investor base is to maintaining the success of a stock?

_____

_____

_____

_____

_____

_____

_____

Have you given any thought to how historical data influences current investing strategies?

_____

_____

_____

_____

_____

_____

_____

Do you feel comfortable reading and recognizing price trends on stock charts?

_____

_____

_____

_____

_____

_____

_____

How frequently do you evaluate your approach based on prior investing successes and failures?

_____

_____

_____

_____

_____

_____

Do you make an effort to absorb lessons from the historical experiences of both successful and failed stocks?

_____

_____

_____

_____

_____

_____

Do you know what hazards there may be in investing without knowing past trends in the stock market?

_____

_____

_____

_____

_____

_____

# EXERCISES

## Interpreting Historical Patterns :

**1**

WHAT DO YOU THINK?

Examine past stock charts to find recurring trends that might help guide current choices.

## Simulation Based on Patterns :

**2**

WHAT DO YOU THINK?

Using historical market data, simulate transactions and use the "Cup with Handle" pattern to get strategic insight.

## Taking Note of Market History:

**3**

WHAT DO YOU THINK?

Examine case studies of businesses that have been influenced by past trends to promote thought-provoking dialogues.

Do you know what hazards there may be in investing without knowing past trends in the stock market?

_____

_____

_____

_____

_____

_____

Do you know what the "handle" of a stock means and how important it is for timing investments?

_____

_____

_____

_____

_____

_____

Do you realize how similar understanding stock market trends is to diagnosing medical conditions?

_____

_____

_____

_____

_____

How often do you use previous stock market movements as seismic data while making decisions?

_____

_____

_____

_____

_____

_____

Have you found any particular examples where a robust investor base affected the durability of a stock?

_____

_____

_____

_____

_____

_____

Do you know what may happen if you buy stocks without having a firm grasp of the past?

_____

_____

_____

_____

_____

_____

# FINAL RESULTS TRACKER

## THE MOST IMPORTANT GOAL I ACHIEVED

## HOW DID I ACHIEVE IT?

## PERSONAL NOTE :

## HOW CAN I KEEP IT UP

## THINGS I'M GRATEFUL FOR:

## LESSONS LEARNED

# CHAPTER 2

## THE MOST CRUCIAL ASPECT OF A SOLID STOCK IS A RISE IN EARNINGS

A basic fact surfaces in the complex world of the stock market: a profitable company is the cornerstone of a successful business, and a profitable company always has a rising stock price. That means that there is just one clear rule to follow when choosing stocks: give preference to those that are showing significant gains in earnings.

The main point, which is that a rising profits is the most crucial characteristic of a quality stock, is clear.

This claim is well supported by historical data, as seen by the development of two major contemporary tech companies, Apple and Google. Google started trading at a low of $85 per share in 2004 and quickly rose to $700 in 2007. At the same time, Apple had a phenomenal increase from $12 to $202 in only 45 months.

Even though both businesses were industry leaders, significant gains in profitability significantly before their rising stock trajectories. Before its stock took off, Google showed profits increases of 112 and 123 percent; in contrast, Apple showed an astounding 350 percent growth in earnings in the quarter before its big jump.

However, this method has risks since the stock market is full of subtleties. A hard lesson learnt during the dotcom bubble of the late 1990s is that investors should avoid the appeal of speculative equities inspired by reports of potential high profitability. A large number of speculative stocks that had no real profits suffered significant losses in the ensuing dotcom bust. On the other hand, financially strong tech companies like AOL and Yahoo! fared far better throughout the storm.

The crucial conclusion emerges: only put money into businesses that have actual, rising profits.

The earnings-per-share (EPS) figure is a crucial indicator that takes center stage in the search for successful businesses. Sensible investors should concentrate on firms with notable, steady percentage improvements in their earnings per share (EPS) figure, which is determined by dividing a company's total after-tax profits by the number of shares issued.

Earnings growth is important, but it shouldn't be the only consideration when choosing stocks to invest in. Other important factors will become clear in the ensuing conversations. The most important aspect impacting the choice to purchase, however, is clearly the percentage growth in EPS.

# Key Lessons

## Lesson 1 : <u>Growth in Earnings as the Foundation</u>

Recognize that a stock's ability to expand its profits is essential, as shown by tech behemoths like Apple and Google.

## Lesson 2 : Preventing Speculation Pitfalls

Take a cue from the dotcom boom and invest only in businesses that have consistent, rising profits to steer clear of such pitfalls.

## Lesson 3 : <u>Pay Attention to Earnings-Per-Share (EPS):</u>

Give top priority to businesses exhibiting notable and stable improvements in EPS

## Lesson 4 : <u>Thorough Decision-Making</u>

Recognize that, while profits growth is important, it shouldn't be the only consideration when making decisions; take other important factors into account as well.

## An investment strategy centered on earnings

NOTE

ACTION PLAN: Create a plan that gives enterprises with actual, increasing profits priority.

ACTION STEPS: Set up a list of requirements for observable profits, add it to your checklist for making investment decisions, and dedicate time to doing research.

## Steer Clear of Speculative Pitfalls

NOTE

ACTION PLAN: Make a checklist to help you steer clear of speculative traps while making investments.

ACTION STEPS: Establish standards for speculative risks, use them to assess possible investments, and monitor how they affect the results of decisions.

## EPS-Driven Investing Strategy

NOTE

ACTION PLAN: Make EPS a priority in your investing strategy.

ACTION STEPS: Establish clear goals for percentage growth in EPS, regularly assess firms in relation to these benchmarks, and adjust your strategy in light of the results.

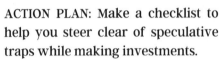

| Goals | Action Plan |
| --- | --- |
|  |  |
|  |  |
|  |  |
|  |  |
|  |  |
|  |  |
|  |  |
|  |  |
|  |  |

## Final Results

Have you realized how crucial profits growth is to a stock's performance?

_____

_____

_____

_____

_____

_____

Do you know of any past instances, like Apple or Google, where large stock increases were preceded by notable increases in earnings?

_____

_____

_____

_____

_____

_____

How often do you give businesses with actual, increasing revenues first priority when making investments?

_____

_____

_____

_____

_____

_____

Have you gained any insight from the dotcom era's speculative stock pitfalls?

_____

_____

_____

_____

_____

_____

_____

Do you actively resist the seduction of hearsay about the possible big returns on speculative stock investments?

_____

_____

_____

_____

_____

_____

_____

Do you know how important the earnings-per-share (EPS) ratio is for assessing how well a business is doing?

_____

_____

_____

_____

_____

_____

_____

How often do you concentrate on businesses that show steady percentage growth in their earnings per share (EPS)?

_____

_____

_____

_____

_____

_____

Have you had difficulties or losses in your investments as a result of undervaluing observable profits?

_____

_____

_____

_____

_____

_____

Do you now invest in businesses that are experiencing significant, actual profit growth?

_____

_____

_____

_____

_____

# EXERCISES

## Analysis of Earnings Growth :

**1**

WHAT DO YOU THINK?

Exercise: Examine the growth patterns of three profitable businesses' profits.

Task: Evaluate and contrast the timing and rate of profits growth with their stock performance.

## Lessons from the Dotcom Era :

**2**

WHAT DO YOU THINK?

Exercises: Examine how speculative stocks performed in the dotcom period.

Task: Examine the relationship between a lack of observable profits and ensuing drops, providing guidance for present investing strategies.

## EPS Assessment :

**3**

WHAT DO YOU THINK?

Exercise: Choose three firms and evaluate the last five years' EPS trends for each.

Task: Recognize trends of steady percentage gains and assess how they relate to the performance of the stock as a whole.

Have you given any thought to how steady EPS growth affects the performance of investments over the long run?

_____

_____

_____

_____

_____

_____

Do you agree that a variety of variables should influence your investing selections, including increase in earnings?

_____

_____

_____

_____

_____

_____

Are you aware of the possible dangers involved in speculating just on future stock market earnings

_____

_____

_____

_____

_____

_____

How often do you examine a company's past record to identify actual increase in earnings?

_____

_____

_____

_____

_____

_____

_____

Have you looked at the paths taken by industry titans like AOL and Yahoo! during the dotcom bust to see what lessons they may share?

_____

_____

_____

_____

_____

_____

_____

Are you prepared to make measurable, steady profits your top priority in your investing plan rather than speculative gains?

_____

_____

_____

_____

_____

_____

# FINAL RESULTS TRACKER

## THE MOST IMPORTANT GOAL I ACHIEVED

## HOW DID I ACHIEVE IT?

## PERSONAL NOTE :

## HOW CAN I KEEP IT UP

## THINGS I'M GRATEFUL FOR:

## LESSONS LEARNED

# CHAPTER 3

## YOU SHOULD KNOW WHEN TO INVEST IN INNOVATIVE FIRMS SINCE THEY MAY PROVIDE A HEALTHY RETURN.

Thomas Edison's incandescent lightbulb and Silicon Valley's digital breakthroughs are just two examples of the disruptive technology that the US has been at the forefront of for more than a century.

The stock market is not immune to this revolutionary force. A thorough analysis of the market's development since 1880 identifies a recurring pattern: businesses that launch ground-breaking innovations often see exponential increases in their stock values. There is no denying the obvious relationship between innovation and successful stock market returns.

The main point is clear: Investing in innovative firms may provide significant returns, but timing is crucial.

Over the years, innovation has repeatedly resulted in impressive gains in stock prices. There are several examples, such as the Northern Pacific's explosive 4,000 percent increase in only two years beginning in 1900 and General Motors' astounding 1,368 percent increase in stock price between 1913 and 1914, which was fueled by the launch of new cars.

One such example is Cisco Systems, which transformed networking by providing hardware that allowed local area networks to be connected.

Between 1990 and 2000, there was a remarkable 75,000% increase in the value of Cisco's shares.

Global innovators are still drawn to the United States because it promises a steady stream of chances similar to those that have been seen in the past. Don't lose hope if you were unable to invest in industry titans like Apple or Microsoft; there will be other opportunities. The secret is to put in the careful work necessary to identify them when the time is right.

But when is the right time? Outstanding, creative businesses often defy conventional wisdom by continuing to develop rapidly and beyond expectations. The adage "buy low, sell high" is untrue; high stock prices do not prevent profitable purchases. Consider Cisco Systems in 1990, which had already reached its peak before seeing an unheard-of 75,000% increase.

Research, like that done by Investor's Business Daily, reveals an unexpected reality: equities that reach new highs during bull market times often continue along this trajectory. On the other hand, stocks that reach new lows keep declining.

However, as was highlighted in the last conversation, there is a smart moment to purchase a stock: when it is about to break out and is consolidating its base. This favorable time can be reliably predicted by the "Cup with Handle" pattern.

The Takeaway:

Seek for outstanding, innovative businesses.
When opportunities arise, such as when the "Cup with Handle" pattern appears, invest in them.
Essentially, the lesson is to strategically position oneself by spotting creative businesses and choosing wisely when to invest depending on time .

# Key Lessons

## Lesson 1 :   **Innovation and Stock Returns**

Recognize that historically, innovation and exponential stock price rise have been correlated.

## Lesson 2 :   **Opportunistic Timing**

Acknowledge the importance of timing while making investments in cutting-edge businesses, stressing the need of choosing the appropriate time.

## Lesson 3 :   **Learn from Past Success Stories**

To help guide current investment choices, consider the lessons learned from the achievements of trailblazing businesses like Northern Pacific, General Motors, and Cisco Systems.

## Lesson 4 :   **The Counterintuitive Nature of High Stocks**

Cisco Systems shows that high stock prices do not always prevent continued exponential development, which challenges conventional thinking.

## Lesson 5 :   **Importance of Strategic Timing**

Gain assurance and comfort while engaging in financial conversations, and recognize the critical role that budgetary concerns play in the decision-making process.

# Action Plan 1 — Action Plan 1

## Investment Strategy Driven by Innovation

**NOTE**

ACTION PLAN: Create an investing strategy that aggressively searches out cutting-edge businesses.

ACTION STEPS: Determine what qualities distinguish creative businesses, add them to your investment checklist, and look for possibilities that fit these requirements.

## The Mastery of Timing Plan

**NOTE**

ACTION PLAN: Draft a guide on how to become an expert at strategically timed investments.

ACTION STEPS: Examine past examples of effective time, include timing into your decision-making process, and adjust your strategy in light of results

## Improvement in Pattern Recognition

**NOTE**

ACTION PLAN: Develop your awareness of strategic patterns, particularly the "Cup with Handle."

ACTION STEPS: To improve your pattern identification abilities, practice identifying patterns, keep up with industry developments, and use knowledge gained from past patterns.

| Goals | Action Plan |
| --- | --- |
|  |  |
|  |  |
|  |  |
|  |  |
|  |  |
|  |  |
|  |  |
|  |  |
|  |  |

## Final Results

Have you given any thought to the past connection between invention and significant increases in stock prices?

_____

_____

_____

_____

_____

_____

_____

Do you understand how crucial time is when making investments in startups?

_____

_____

_____

_____

_____

_____

_____

How frequently do you base your investing strategy on the past achievements of companies like Northern Pacific, General Motors, and Cisco Systems?

_____

_____

_____

_____

_____

Are you willing to reconsider the conventional knowledge around current high stock prices and their prospects for further appreciation?

_____

_____

_____

_____

_____

_____

_____

Have you actively looked for chances to invest in cutting-edge businesses while using the knowledge from the past?

_____

_____

_____

_____

_____

_____

_____

Even if a stock seems to be at a peak, do you think you can still spot the right time to buy in it?

_____

_____

_____

_____

_____

_____

_____

How often do you use stock patterns such as the "Cup with Handle" analysis to guide your investing decisions?

_____

_____

_____

_____

_____

_____

Have you had trouble figuring out when to invest in startups that are doing things differently?

_____

_____

_____

_____

_____

_____

Do you draw conclusions from seemingly contradictory patterns, like equities reaching new highs and continuing to rise?

_____

_____

_____

_____

_____

# EXERCISES

## Analysis of Innovative Companies :

**Exercises:** Select three forward-thinking businesses and examine their past stock price increases.

**Activity:** Find trends or elements that make them successful, then use these understandings to assess available investment possibilities.

## Workshop on Historical Patterns :

**Exercise:** Plan a workshop on historical stock trends with an emphasis on companies such as Cisco Systems, General Motors, and Northern Pacific.

**Activity:** Invite participants to debate possible tactics and make comparisons with current market circumstances.

## Simulating strategic timing:

**Exercise:** Use historical stock data to simulate the timing of strategic investments.

**Task:** Utilize the "Cup with Handle" pattern and evaluate results to enhance your comprehension of tactical timing.

Have you looked at how past data on firms reaching all-time highs in bull markets affects the way you make investments?

_____

_____

_____

_____

_____

_____

Even if you passed up chances to invest with industry titans like Apple or Microsoft, are you actively looking for cutting-edge businesses to support?

_____

_____

_____

_____

_____

_____

How frequently do you think back on what may be learnt about speculative investments from the dotcom era?

_____

_____

_____

_____

_____

Do you know about the constant flow of creative people coming to the US and the potential that this has created for the stock market?

Have you given careful thought to how finding cutting-edge businesses at the ideal moment to invest in them can benefit from diligence?

Do you evaluate equities using a comprehensive strategy that considers things like breakout patterns and consolidation?

# FINAL RESULTS
# TRACKER

## THE MOST IMPORTANT GOAL I ACHIEVED

## HOW DID I ACHIEVE IT?

## PERSONAL NOTE :

## HOW CAN I KEEP IT UP

## THINGS I'M GRATEFUL FOR:

## LESSONS LEARNED

# CHAPTER 4

## WHEN CHOOSING STOCKS, SUPPLY AND DEMAND PLAY A a SIGNIFICANT ROLE

The price of almost everything is influenced by the fine balance of supply and demand in the complex dance of market dynamics, from everyday necessities like cheese and toothpaste to stationary products. It should come as no surprise that this basic idea has an impact on the complicated world of the stock market.

The main point—that supply and demand play a significant role in stock selection—resonates.

Imagine a situation in which one business offers 5 billion shares, whereas another chooses to issue just 50 million. This is when supply and demand dynamics come into play. In order to accomplish a meaningful stock rise for the corporation that owns 5 billion shares, a massive amount of purchasing is required. On the other hand, a smaller company with only 50 million shares may see sharp price fluctuations due to quick increases in demand.

But more volatility goes hand in hand with this possibility of a quick climb. Even if a "small-cap" stock has the potential to provide enormous returns, it also has the potential to fall spectacularly. In contrast, a corporation with a higher number of issued shares is considered less hazardous since it takes significant selling to affect price changes.

Thus, a smaller business may provide more spectacular returns, while a bigger business may give a more dependable, albeit less spectacular, investment. This is because of the rule of supply and demand. In this case, ownership structure is quite important. The ownership of a significant portion of the company's shares by senior management is a favorable sign for both big and small businesses. On the other hand, the stock may represent a liability in a portfolio if management does not have a significant stake in the company's success. In general, an investment is more appealing if management holds a minimum of 1 to 3 percent of a major company and a larger share of smaller businesses.

The choice of a business to repurchase its own shares, which is seen as a favorable indicator, is another important consideration. This calculated move indicates the company's expectation of faster-than-expected profits growth and more demand for its shares.

Comprehending the complicated relationship between supply and demand, together with thoughtful analysis of ownership structures and tactical buybacks, enables investors to make better informed decisions while navigating the intricacies of stock markets.

# Key Lessons

## Lesson 1 : **Market Dynamics Revealed**

Understand how supply and demand, like those affecting daily commodities, play a crucial part in determining stock values.

## Lesson 2 : **Volatility and Reward Correlation**

Recognize the trade-off between volatility and possible rewards, and acknowledge the relationship between a company's share quantity and the possibility of swift, dramatic price fluctuations.

## Lesson 3 : **Assessing risk**

Assessing risk and ensuring the reliability of investments requires an understanding of the benefits and drawbacks of investing in small and large-cap stocks. While bigger firms may provide a more steady investment, smaller companies may give more explosive returns.

## Lesson 4 : **Significance of Ownership Structure**

Acknowledge the significance of senior management ownership, since a sizable share indicates a vested interest in the company's performance and increases the investment's appeal.

**Action Plan 1** — — **Action Plan 1** — — **Action Plan 1**

### The strategy of diversification

ACTION PLAN: Formulate a plan that strikes a balance between small- and large-cap stock investing.

ACTION STEPS: Establish diversification criteria, assign a portion of your portfolio to each area, and periodically reevaluate in light of changing market conditions.

**NOTE**

### Checklist for Ownership Evaluation

ACTION PLAN: Make a list of questions to ask prospective investors about their ownership arrangements.

ACTION STEPS: Establish the parameters for advantageous ownership arrangements, use the checklist while conducting the study, and make adjustments in light of the results.

**NOTE**

### Integration of Strategic Buyback

ACTION PLAN: Make strategic buybacks an integral part of your investing strategy.

ACTION STEPS: Keep up with corporations that are buying back their stock, evaluate their justifications, and use this knowledge to your decision-making.

**NOTE**

| Goals | Action Plan |
| --- | --- |
|  |  |
|  |  |
|  |  |
|  |  |
|  |  |
|  |  |
|  |  |
|  |  |
|  |  |

## Final Results

Have you thought about how supply and demand affect stock prices and made comparisons to other common commodities?

_____

_____

_____

_____

_____

_____

_____

Do you know whether there is a trade-off between the number of shares a firm has and the probability of significant price fluctuations?

_____

_____

_____

_____

_____

_____

How often do you weigh the benefits and hazards of investing in small- and large-cap stocks?

_____

_____

_____

_____

_____

_____

Do you see the connection between more volatility and a smaller company's potential for spectacular results?

_____

_____

_____

_____

_____

_____

Have there been cases when smaller businesses produced greater returns in spite of the associated volatility?

_____

_____

_____

_____

_____

_____

Are you willing to consider the possibility that investing possibilities in bigger, maybe less spectacular firms could be more stable?

_____

_____

_____

_____

_____

To what extent do you examine
ownership structures in detail,
particularly the portion of shares
held by upper management?

_____

_____

_____

_____

_____

_____

_____

Do you think that a company's
management ownership has a
significant impact on how
successful you think it can be?

_____

_____

_____

_____

_____

_____

_____

When making investing
selections, are you comfortable
differentiating between
companies that have a high and
low level of management
ownership?

_____

_____

_____

_____

# EXERCISES

## Analysis of Supply and Demand

**Exercise: Examine past stock price changes in relation to supply and demand dynamics.**

**Task: Recognize trends and patterns to improve your comprehension of how these dynamics affect stock values.**

## Simulating Risk and Reward :

**Exercise: To better understand the risks and benefits associated with investing in small and large-cap companies, simulate your investments.**

**Activity: Assess the results and make deductions to guide your investment choices and risk tolerance**

## Case Studies on Ownership Structures :

**Task: Investigate and examine the ownership arrangements of businesses across various industries.**

**Activity: In a group environment, discuss case studies and make connections between ownership arrangements and the success of the whole firm.**

How often do your evaluations take into account the importance of a company's choice to repurchase its own stock?

_____

_____

_____

_____

_____

_____

_____

Have you looked into how a repurchase of shares can affect the demand for the company's stock and future earnings?

_____

_____

_____

_____

_____

_____

_____

When assessing investing prospects, are you aware of how supply and demand dynamics affect stock price movements?

_____

_____

_____

_____

_____

_____

How frequently do you consider the benefits and dangers that come with owning various kinds of equities in your portfolio?

_____

_____

_____

_____

_____

_____

_____

Have you ever seen the potential rewards of taking on the volatility of investing in tiny businesses that are growing at an exponential rate?

_____

_____

_____

_____

_____

_____

_____

In pursuing your investing objectives, are you ready to negotiate the trade-offs between volatility and stability?

_____

_____

_____

_____

_____

_____

# FINAL RESULTS TRACKER

## THE MOST IMPORTANT GOAL  I ACHIEVED

## HOW DID I ACHIEVE IT?

## PERSONAL NOTE :

## HOW CAN I KEEP IT UP

## THINGS I'M GRATEFUL FOR:

## LESSONS LEARNED

# CHAPTER 5

## INVEST IN SECTOR LEADERS

Among the plethora of investment options available, we tend to choose well-known brands that arouse good feelings, like Nike or Coca-Cola. These are the businesses that speak to us and compel us to think about making an investment in them. But sometimes, when exciting new leaders emerge, the characteristics of a bull market might cause these old favorites to fall behind.

The takeaway is quite clear: You should invest in industry leaders.

Investing in the top businesses in their respective industry is a tried-and-true method when used as a guide. Despite popular belief, a "leading company" isn't always the biggest or most well-known brand. Rather, these are the businesses that have the strongest sales growth, widest profit margins, highest return on equity, and the greatest quarterly and yearly profits growth. Crucially, the exceptional success of these organizations is propelled by a distinctive and inventive product.

It's clear from looking back at the author's own accomplishments that great victors tended to become dominant figures in the business. From Pick 'N' Save (1976–1983) to Apple (2004–2007), Amgen (1990–1991), AOL (1998–1999), eBay (2002–2004), and AOL (1998–1999), each company solidly held the top spot in their respective industries.

The message is clear: Investing in these innovative businesses is always preferable than purchasing nostalgic old favorites.

This is best shown by looking at the past bull market of 1979 and 1980. Dynamic firms like Burroughs and IBM saw a relative stagnation while dynamic firms like Wang Labs, Tandy, and Datapoint saw rises of up to seven times. The industry leaders did not deliver the enormous returns that were expected, despite the old favorites' track record of dependability over time.

A warning is issued against investing in imitation or subpar businesses. Usually, the industry leader does better than its competitors. It is seldom profitable to invest with the expectation that a secondary company would benefit from the market leader's shine.

In the wise words of businessman Andrew Carnegie, "The first man gets the oyster; the second, the shell." The true innovators and entrepreneurs are the ones who propel the market. These are the businesses that are worthy of notice and funding consideration.

The main takeaway is straightforward: Make strategic investments by selecting market leaders that have a history of domination and innovation.

# Key Lessons

## Lesson 1 :   strategic investment

Prioritize industry leaders based on predetermined criteria, such as strong sales growth, broad profit margins, high return on equity, and powerful profits growth, to acknowledge the significance of strategic investment.

## Lesson 2 : Innovation as a Driving Force

Acknowledge that the innovative and entrepreneurial spirit of industry leaders is frequently what makes them stand out in the marketplace via their ground-breaking and distinctive goods.

## Lesson 3 :   Historical Success Patterns

Take a cue from past achievements and realize that businesses at the top of their respective fields often generate large profits, outperforming personal favorites in a competitive market.

## Lesson 4 :   Be Wary of Copycat Investments

Be wary of investing in second-rate or copycat businesses as the real market leaders often succeed, and secondary players seldom benefit from the apparent luster.

## Action Plan 1 — Action Plan 1

### Integration of Strategic Investment Criteria

**NOTE**

ACTION PLAN: Include certain investment criteria in your decision-making process, including profit margins and profits growth.

ACTION STEPS: Create a set of standards, apply it to possible investments, and then make adjustments in light of the results.

### Leader in the Industry's Exploration Approach

**NOTE**

ACTION PLAN: Create a plan for aggressively searching for and identifying leading companies across a range of industries.

Action STEPS: Look into the leading firms in each of your sectors, evaluate their track records, and make any necessary changes to your investment portfolio.

### The Innovation Integration Blueprint

**NOTE**

ACTION PLAN: Draft a plan outlining how you will include innovation concerns into your investing approach.

ACTION STEPS: Keep yourself updated on new goods and methods, actively look for possibilities that fit in with these innovations, and review your plan of action in light of how innovation is affecting the leadership in your sector.

| Goals | Action Plan |
| --- | --- |
| | |
| | |
| | |
| | |
| | |
| | |
| | |
| | |
| | |

## Final Results

| |
| --- |
| |
| |
| |
| |

When evaluating possible investments, do you give certain factors, such as profit margins and profits growth, top priority?

How often do you actively look for cutting-edge businesses offering distinctive items to invest in for the long term?

Are you willing to change your attention from personally meaningful favorites to successful industry leaders?

Are you aware of the relationship that exists between a business's potential for large profits and its position as the industry leader?

_____

_____

_____

_____

_____

_____

_____

Have there been times when the dynamic enterprises in your investing portfolio have fared better than the established giants?

_____

_____

_____

_____

_____

_____

_____

Considering that sector leaders have historically outperformed second-rate or imitation enterprises, are you wary of investing in them?

_____

_____

_____

_____

_____

When making investment choices, how often do you evaluate a company's creativity and entrepreneurial spirit?

_____
_____
_____

_____
_____
_____
_____

Do you actively look for past performance trends in market leaders' businesses to inform your investing strategy?

_____
_____
_____

_____
_____
_____
_____

Are you aware of how the dynamics of the market may change during bull markets, when it's possible for new leaders to overtake long-standing favorites?

_____
_____
_____
_____

# EXERCISES

## CAnalysis of Supply and Demand :

**Exercise: Research businesses that are renowned for being leaders in their respective fields.**

**Activity: Examine the elements that have contributed to their success, focusing on important parameters including sales growth, profit margins, return on equity, and profits growth.**

## Sentimentality and Performance Evaluation :

**Exercise: Compare the success of industry leaders with emotional favorites.**

**Task: Examine the results and think about modifying your investing strategy in light of the noted variations.**

## Workshop on Innovation Identification :

**Exercise: Set up a workshop to find cutting-edge goods and methods across many sectors.**

**Activity: Based on the discoveries that have been made and their possible influence on the leadership of the sector, talk about possible investment prospects.**

How do you handle this part of
your investing journey, and have
you had any difficulties
discovering industry leaders?

_____

_____

_____

_____

_____

_____

_____

Are you able to tell the difference
between businesses that are
growing their revenues quickly
and those who are dependent on
sentimentality?

_____

_____

_____

_____

_____

_____

How often do you think about
how new goods affect a business's
overall success and position in the
market?

_____

_____

_____

_____

_____

_____

Have you thought about how your investing approach has changed as a result of the past successes of businesses like Apple, eBay, Amgen, AOL, Pick 'N' Save, and Amgen?

Are you prepared to put nostalgic favorites aside and look at prospects with forward-thinking business leaders?

When making investing selections, do you proactively look for information on a company's return on equity and other important metrics?

# FINAL RESULTS TRACKER

## THE MOST IMPORTANT GOAL I ACHIEVED

## HOW DID I ACHIEVE IT?

## PERSONAL NOTE :

## HOW CAN I KEEP IT UP

## THINGS I'M GRATEFUL FOR:

## LESSONS LEARNED

# CHAPTER 6

## SEEK FOR COMPANIES THAT HAVE INSTITUTIONAL SUPPORT.

In the complex world of investing, some decide against buying individual shares and instead aggregate their money into funds. These group investment vehicles, referred to as mutual funds in the US, are overseen by large organizations under the direction of financial professionals who carefully choose the equities that are included. It becomes essential for individual stock investors to investigate the stocks selected by these financial specialists.

The main takeaway is still relevant today: seek for equities backed by institutions.

These powerful organizations control a large portion of the world's stock purchases, influencing stock prices and market trends. As such, keeping a careful eye on what they do turns into a calculated move. Possessing shares that these organizations support often leads to a portfolio's upward trajectory.

The actions of the top-performing funds, which are managed by astute investors and produce significant yearly returns, are especially important. Investor's Business Daily and Morningstar.com, among other resources, present comprehensive profiles of these funds' top holdings and offer insights into the performance of these funds.

It is important to comprehend institutional investment regardless of whether it originates from high-performing funds.

When numerous funds invest in a given company, their combined influence usually drives up the stock's value.

Examining the institutional stance on stock selection provides insightful information beyond just monitoring their actions. The greatest source of information for potential investors is the fund prospectuses, which may be downloaded or requested directly. These papers describe the strategies and stock selections made by each fund.

However, the situation of major institutions being "over-owned" in equities is urged to be avoided. Certain equities could be bought for you automatically, even if their financial standing is in doubt. The case study of Xerox throughout the 1970s is a sobering reminder. Though it was favored by organizations with a strong track record, shrewd analysts found underlying problems, which caused the stock to drop.

The most important takeaway summarizes the fundamentals of strategic investing: Take advice from the experts, but supplement it with your own research.

To sum up, there are a lot of options available in the complex dance of institutional sponsorship in the stock market. Although it might be beneficial to follow the lead of large organizations, the real strength comes from combining this knowledge with independent investigation and diligence to create a comprehensive and well-informed investment plan.

# Key Lessons

## Lesson 1 : **Impact of Institutional Endorsement**

Recognize the possibility for favorable portfolio results when aligning with their stock selections, and grasp the substantial influence that institutional sponsorship has on stock prices and market dynamics.

## Lesson 2 : **Strategic Attention to Top-Performing Funds**

Recognize how important it is to keep an eye on the operations of top-performing funds and ask investors who regularly produce significant yearly returns for advice.

## Lesson 3 : **Using Resources to Gain Insights**

To help individual investors make well-informed decisions, make use of resources such as Investor's Business Daily and Morningstar.com to gain insightful information on the top holdings and activities of institutional funds.

## Lesson 4 : **Philosophical Understanding of Institutional Investors**

Acknowledge the significance of exploring institutional investors' philosophies when selecting companies, and glean insightful information about their methods and favored stock categories from fund prospectuses.

**Action Plan 1**

**Action Plan 1**

**Action Plan 1**

TAKE ACTION ✓

NOTE

We Deliberately Left This Part Blank. Feel free to Set All the Goals the Suit you Here.

TAKE ACTION ✓

NOTE

TAKE ACTION ✓

NOTE

| Goals | Action Plan |
| --- | --- |
|  |  |
|  |  |
|  |  |
|  |  |
|  |  |
|  |  |
|  |  |
|  |  |
|  |  |

## Final Results

Has your investing plan taken into account how institutional sponsorship affects stock prices and market movements?

_____

_____

_____

_____

_____

_____

_____

How often do you keep a close eye on the top-performing funds' operations to learn about possible investment opportunities?

_____

_____

_____

_____

_____

_____

Have you looked at institutional investors' approach to stock selection, paying special attention to their methods and favorite stock categories?

_____

_____

_____

_____

_____

_____

Taking into account the possible hazards connected with automated buying, are you wary of investing in equities that large institutions could "over-own"?

How often do you make investments in equities that get attention from different funds because you know they have the potential to appreciate in value?

Do you actively look for ways to build a well-rounded investing plan by fusing institutional knowledge with your own research?

Have you ever had good portfolio results by sticking with equities that institutional investors have recommended?

_____

_____

_____

_____

_____

_____

_____

Are you willing to adjust your investing strategy in light of lessons learned from the top-performing funds' activities?

_____

_____

_____

_____

_____

_____

_____

How often do you review your investing strategy in light of changes in market conditions and institutional endorsement patterns?

_____

_____

_____

_____

_____

# EXERCISES

## Analysis of Institutional Impact :

**1**

WHAT DO YOU THINK?

Exercise: Examine past data to see how institutional sponsorship affects certain companies.

Task: Recognize patterns and trends to help you better understand how institutional support affects stock prices.

## Simulating an Institutional Portfolio :

**2**

WHAT DO YOU THINK?

Exercise: Play the role of assembling an investing portfolio from the top institutional funds that are currently performing.

Task: Assess the simulated results and make inferences about the possible advantages of supporting institutional decisions.

## Workshop on Stock-Picking Philosophy :

**3**

WHAT DO YOU THINK?

Exercise: Set up a workshop to investigate various institutional funds' approaches to selecting stocks.

Activity: Talk about the results in a group environment and make connections between stock-picking theories and past fund performance.

Will you proactively look for ways to improve your comprehension of how institutional sponsorship affects certain companies in your portfolio?

Have you had trouble striking a balance between the requirement for independent investigation and due diligence and your dependence on institutional guidance?

Are you comfortable pointing out possible hazards connected to equities that large institutions could be "over-owning"?

In particular, how do you assess
institutional fund activities in
terms of how they affect stock
prices and market dynamics?

_____

_____

_____

_____

_____

_____

Have you looked at past cases
when equities had fallen even
with institutional support? If
yes, what conclusions did you
make from such cases?

_____

_____

_____

_____

_____

_____

How do you incorporate
knowledge of possible biases into
your investing strategy and are
you aware that they might affect
institutional decisions?

_____

_____

_____

_____

_____

# FINAL RESULTS
# TRACKER

## THE MOST IMPORTANT GOAL  I ACHIEVED

## HOW DID I ACHIEVE IT?

## PERSONAL NOTE :

## HOW CAN I KEEP IT UP

## THINGS I'M GRATEFUL FOR:

## LESSONS LEARNED

# CHAPTER 7

## YOU SHOULD CLOSELY MONITOR THE OVERALL TRAJECTORY OF THE MARKET

Within the complex realm of investment, individual equities have little relevance. Unfortunately, most equities will see a decrease in value if the market as a whole has a slump. This sends a very obvious and important message: You should closely monitor the overall direction of the market.

However, just what does the "general market" consist of? In general, it includes a thorough rundown of the main stock indexes, which are easily available online and include the S&P 500, the Dow Jones Industrial Average, and the Nasdaq Composite.

In order to determine the overall sentiment of the market, investors should determine whether there are any noteworthy purchasing or selling actions taking place. Through an Accumulation/Distribution Rating for indexes like the Nasdaq, resources like Investor's Business Daily provide insightful information regarding investor confidence or fears about a probable decline.

It is critical to keep an eye on these indicators since market mood may change in a matter of weeks. Investors might be taken by surprise by a significant market meltdown if they don't maintain their vigilance. For example, regular patterns in the opening high and closing low of stocks may indicate the start of a bear market, while the opposite tendency may indicate the start of a bull market. Without regular observation, these significant changes may go overlooked.

Contrary to popular belief, depending too much on newsletters or financial gurus might result in expensive diversions. These alleged "experts" are less trustworthy sources of information since their differing viewpoints often cause confusion rather than clarity. The best course of action is to examine the market itself; this is similar to researching wildlife by seeing the animals in their natural environment.

As a comparison, think of the study of tigers. Although there is a wealth of material about tigers, nothing can quite match the educational benefit of seeing the creatures for oneself in their natural habitat. In a similar vein, the most enlightening lessons about the wild world of the stock market come from seeing its ups and downs firsthand.

Essentially, the advice given to investors is to become keen observers of the market, depending less on the divergent viewpoints of experts and more on personal observations. Similar to monitoring animals, traversing the wilderness of the stock market demands acute awareness, enabling investors to interpret the signals and make well-informed judgments based on the dynamically changing nature of the market.

# Key Lessons

## Lesson 1 : **Market's Predominant Power**

Recognize that the whole market has a significant impact on the performance of individual stocks, and stress how important it is to keep an eye on larger market patterns

## Lesson 2 : **Summary of the Principal Indices**

Recognize the importance of leading stock indexes as gauges of the general direction of the market, such as the S&P 500, Dow Jones Industrial Average, and Nasdaq Composite.

## Lesson 3 : **Indicators of Investor Confidence**

Acknowledge the usefulness of instruments such as Investor's Business Daily's Accumulation/Distribution Rating in assessing investor mood and confidence on current market circumstances.

## Lesson 4 : **Prompt Response to Changes in the Market**

Stress that market indices should be watched carefully and promptly since changes may happen quickly and have an effect on investment portfolios.

## Action Plan 1

### Integrated Procedure for Market Observation

**NOTE**

Establish a consistent practice of integrated market monitoring, including the use of instruments such as the Accumulation/Distribution Rating and key index tracking.

### Using a Variety of Information Sources

**NOTE**

Expand the range of sources from which you get market data, going beyond newsletters and financial experts.

### The Blueprint for Continuous Learning and Adaptation

**NOTE**

Using first hand market observation, develop a roadmap for ongoing learning and modification.

| Goals | Action Plan |
| --- | --- |
|  |  |
|  |  |
|  |  |
|  |  |
|  |  |
|  |  |
|  |  |
|  |  |
|  |  |

## Final Results

Have you given any thought to how broad market fluctuations can affect your specific stock investments?

_____

_____

_____

_____

_____

_____

_____

How often do you actively track significant stock indexes to evaluate general market movements, such as the S&P 500, Dow Jones, and Nasdaq?

_____

_____

_____

_____

_____

_____

_____

Do you know how important it is to use tools like the Accumulation/Distribution Rating to determine how investors feel about certain indices?

_____

_____

_____

_____

Have there been times when keeping an eye on market indices in real time allowed you to respond to changes in the market effectively?

_____

_____

_____

_____

_____

_____

_____

Can you use consistent monitoring of stock activity to clearly identify patterns that indicate a bull or bear market?

_____

_____

_____

_____

_____

_____

_____

Do you often see patterns in which equities start high and close low, perhaps indicating a bear market?

_____

_____

_____

_____

_____

_____

_____

Do you know about the other
tendency, in which equities open
poorly and finish strongly,
perhaps signaling the start of a
bull market?

How often do you examine
market indices to make sure you
are not taken aback by abrupt
changes in the dynamics of the
market?

Regarding your investing
selections, have you found the
newsletters and views of financial
experts to be clear or confusing?

# EXERCISES

### Simulation of Market Indices :

- **Practice:** Follow the main market indexes for a predetermined amount of time.
- **Task:** Examine simulated trends to find trends and possible changes that point to bull or bear markets.

---

## Workshop on Tool Utilisation :

- **Task:** Lead a session on the use of instruments such as the Accumulation/Distribution Rating.
- **Practice** analyzing ratings for different indexes and talking about how they affect market conditions and investor sentiment.

---

## Comparative Evaluation: Market vs. Wildlife

- **Exercise:** Compare and contrast watching animals with watching the financial market.
- **Activity:** Talk about ways to develop your market observation abilities by using lessons learned from the natural world

Do you see the similarity
between closely monitoring the
financial market and animals to
make better informed decisions?

How can you improve your
strategy such that it more closely
resembles the best practice of
direct market observation?

Will you make future investing
selections based more on in-
person market observation than
just financial pundits?

In order to improve your investing strategy, are you willing to look at information sources other than financial experts and newsletters?

Have there been times when the success of particular stocks in your portfolio was overshadowed by the overall market's influence?

Currently, how do you use the knowledge gained from direct market observation to your whole investing approach?

# FINAL RESULTS TRACKER

## THE MOST IMPORTANT GOAL  I ACHIEVED

## HOW DID I ACHIEVE IT?

## PERSONAL NOTE :

## HOW CAN I KEEP IT UP

## THINGS I'M GRATEFUL FOR:

## LESSONS LEARNED

# FINAL SUMMARY: SOLVING THE STOCK MARKET MYSTERIES

Key takeaways from these insight are clear:

Understanding Stock-Price Trends:

Key emphasis: Make understanding stock-price patterns a top priority. Pay close attention to the important "Cup with Handle" pattern in particular.

Comprehensive Stock Evaluation:

Important Point to Remember: Evaluate your selected stock carefully in addition to looking at trends. Make certain that it is a market leader, that it offers cutting-edge goods or services, and—above all—that its profits have been rising steadily.

Innovation and Sector Leadership:

Key Point: Invest in firms that are leaders in their sectors and, preferably, provide cutting-edge solutions. The market's potential for resilience and steady expansion is increased by this combination.

Growth in Earnings as a Foundation:

Crucial Pillar: Find companies that have shown a significant rise in profits. This element is fundamental to an investment's soundness and often serves as a forecast for future performance.

Fund managers' pearls of wisdom:

Crucial Takeaway: Pay great attention to the actions of leading fund managers to get understanding of their investing choices. But counterbalance this with your own investigation and due diligence.

Fund managers' pearls of wisdom:

Crucial Takeaway: Pay great attention to the actions of leading fund managers to get understanding of their investing choices. But counterbalance this with your own investigation and due diligence.

Individual Carefulness:

Key Instruction: Recognize the indispensable importance of independent study and careful diligence while picking the brains of experienced fund managers. It acts as a barrier against mindlessly adhering to market trends.

All things considered, these observations provide a thorough manual for anybody venturing into the complex realm of stock market investing. Investors can navigate the complexities of the market with greater confidence and informed decision-making if they can master the art of reading stock-price patterns, ensure holistic stock health, prioritize industry leadership and innovation, emphasize earnings growth, and strike a balance between expert insights and personal due diligence.

Useful Advice: Strategically Reduce Losses!

Knowing when to join and when to leave the stock market is just as important as understanding when to enter. This information acts as a safeguard against large monetary losses. Generally speaking, you should think about selling a stock if its value drops below 8 percent of what you paid when you first bought it. Following this approach successfully reduces your losses and provides a buffer as you seek potentially large rewards. A balanced and responsible investing plan is ensured by this methodical approach to loss reduction.